PAUL FELL'S

TRUE NEBRASKANS

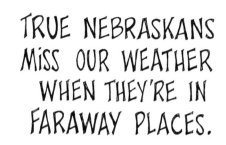

TRUE NEBRASKANS REALLY HATE TO LOSE.

TRUE NEBRASKANS BELIEVE
THEMSELVES TO BE HANDY
AROUND THE HOUSE.

TRUE NEBRASKANS KNOW
THERE ARE TWO KINDS
OF CATS.

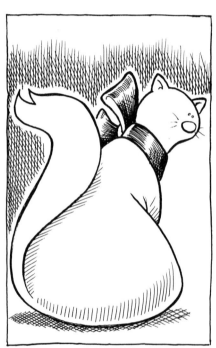

DOMESTIC AND FARM.

NEVER CUT IN FRONT OF
A TRUE NEBRASKAN
IN A BUFFET LINE.

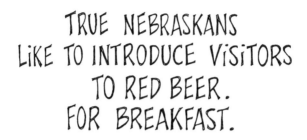

TRUE NEBRASKANS
LiKE TO INTRODUCE ViSiTORS
TO RED BEER.
FOR BREAKFAST.

TRUE NEBRASKANS
CAN SPOT A POLITICIAN
A MILE AWAY.

TRUE NEBRASKANS KNOW
THAT WHOEVER INVENTED
THE WIND CHILL INDEX

NEVER HAD TO DO
WINTER CHORES.

TRUE NEBRASKANS
LiVE LONGER THAN
MOST AMERiCANS.

USUALLY OUT OF SPiTE.

TRUE NEBRASKANS LIKE TO
SIT IN THE BLEACHERS
AND HOLLER AND CHEER.

WHEN FAMILY MEMBERS GRADUATE.

TRUE NEBRASKANS LIKE TO TAKE OUT-OF-STATERS GOLFING.

ON COURSES WITH SAND GREENS.

TRUE NEBRASKANS BELIEVE
YOU CAN HAUL AS MANY
PEOPLE IN A PICKUP
AS YOU CAN IN A CAR.

TRUE NEBRASKANS
SOMETIMES FIND IT USEFUL
TO HAVE A LAWYER
IN THE FAMILY.

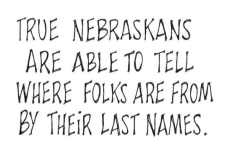

TRUE NEBRASKANS WHO LIVE
OUT IN THE COUNTRY
KEEP A DOG FOR PROTECTION.

MORE OR LESS.

TRUE NEBRASKANS THINK
T.V. HAS GONE TO HELL
SINCE THEY MOVED
THE WEATHER REPORT
OUT OF THE LEADOFF SLOT
ON THE EVENING NEWS.

TRUE NEBRASKANS THINK
THE 4 BASIC FOOD GROUPS ARE:
STEAK. RIBS.
HAMBURGER. PORK CHOPS.

TRUE NEBRASKANS ARE WiLLiNG TO LEAVE TAKING PiCTURES OF TORNADOES TO THE CiTY FOLKS.

TO TRUE NEBRASKANS,
THE DIFFERENCE BETWEEN
A BARBER AND A HAIR STYLIST
IS ABOUT 10 BUCKS.

TRUE NEBRASKANS
ARE GREAT BELIEVERS
IN EQUAL OPPORTUNITY.

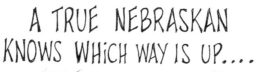

A TRUE NEBRASKAN
KNOWS WHICH WAY IS UP....

TRUE NEBRASKANS
DON'T CONSIDER DOGS
TO BE JUST PETS.

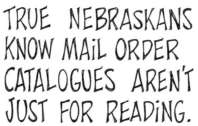

TRUE NEBRASKANS
KNOW MAIL ORDER
CATALOGUES AREN'T
JUST FOR READING.

© PAUL FELL

TRUE NEBRASKANS MOVE
INTO THE INFORMATION AGE WHILE
KEEPING TRADITIONAL VALUES.

TRUE NEBRASKANS KNOW
THAT FEW DEMOCRATS
LIVE OUT IN THE THIRD
CONGRESSIONAL DISTRICT.

HE WAS A
PURTY GOOD
OL' BOY....

FOR A LIBERAL,
THAT IS....

REST IN PEACE

THEY DIE OF LONELINESS.

MANY TRUE NEBRASKANS
HAVE NO DESIRE
TO LIVE BACK EAST.

THEY CAN'T WAIT FOR
THE T.V. NEWS & WEATHER
AT 11 P.M.

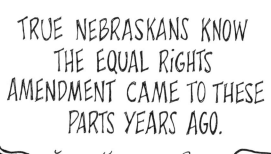

TRUE NEBRASKANS LIKE TO TRAVEL.

SMOOCH!

IT HELPS THEM APPRECIATE BEING BACK HOME.